T0153282

Blessed Names and Characteristics of The Prophet Muḥammad ﷺ

Blessed Names and Characteristics

of

The Prophet ﷺ Muḥammad

Abdur Raheem Kidwai

First published in England by

Kube Publishing Ltd
Markfield Conference Centre
Ratby Lane, Markfield,
Leicestershire LE67 9SY
United Kingdom
Tel: +44 (0) 1530 249230
Fax: +44 (0) 1530 249656
Website: www.kubepublishing.com
Email: info@kubepublishing.com

2nd impression, 2020

Cataloguing-in-Publication Data
is available from the British Library

ISBN 978 1 84774 088 5 *casebound*
ISBN 978 1 84774 092 2 *Box set edition*

Typeset N.A. Qaddoura
Design Imtiaze Ahmed
Printed Mega Basim, Turkey

CONTENTS

TRANSLITERATION TABLE

Arabic Consonants

Initial, unexpressed medial and final: ء ’

ا	a	د	d	ض	ḍ	ك	k
ب	b	ذ	dh	ط	ṭ	ل	l
ت	t	ر	r	ظ	ẓ	م	m
ث	th	ز	z	ع	‘	ن	n
ج	j	س	s	غ	gh	ه	h
ح	ḥ	ش	sh	ف	f	و	w
خ	kh	ص	ṣ	ق	q	ي	y

With a *shaddah*, both medial and final consonants are doubled.

Vowels, diphthongs, etc.

Short:	ـَ	a	ـِ	i	ـُ	u
Long:	ـَا	ā	ـِي	ī	ـُو	ū
Diphthongs:			ـَوْ	aw		
			ـَيْ	ay		

PREFACE

The Prophet Muḥammad (peace be upon him) occupies a pivotal position in the Islamic scheme of things. This work is intended to enable readers to gain a better idea of the many brilliant facets of the Prophet's personality and accomplishments. For this compendium contains the elucidation of his 99 excellent names and attributes. Since these names, both personal and attributive, feature in the Qur'ān and Ḥadīth collections, their importance hardly calls for any further elaboration.

This work represents a sequel to the Kube publication, *Blessed Names and Attributes of Allah* which lists and elucidates 99 excellent names and attributes of Allah. It has been my endeavour to explain in simple, easy to understand English, the excellent names and attributes of the Prophet (peace be upon him) with a view to drawing attention to his various noble roles and laudable traits. Moreover, this study should help readers grasp better the Prophet's centrality in Islam and the interrelationship between Allah, the Prophet Muḥammad (peace be upon him) and believers. Needless to add, the Prophet's names are reflective of his impeccable character and conduct and his exalted rank. Thus, this study may inspire us further to emulate the role model embodied by him. Since the Prophet Muḥammad (peace be upon him) is the Final Messenger of Allah, his example is valid and relevant until the Last Day. This should make us all the more keen on studying and following the Prophet's glorious example in all aspects of our life, both individual and collective. This description of the Prophet's excellent names and attributes may also familiarize readers with a basic article of Islamic faith: the institution of Prophethood.

I am thankful to the Kube team: Brothers Haris Ahmad, Yahya Birt, and Mohammad Siddique Seddon for reposing trust in me for writing this book. Words fail me in thanking Dr M Manazir Ahsan, of the Islamic Foundation, Leicester, for his valuable input which ensured the accuracy of this work. The credit for typesetting and production goes to Br Naiem Qaddoura, also Br Imtiaze Ahmed for Cover design and template. May Allah reward all of them.

I hope this work will be successful in achieving the above mentioned objectives. May Allah make it a source of our guidance and enlightenment. (Āmīn)

Abdur Raheem Kidwai
Professor, Department of English
Aligarh Muslim University, India
Muḥarram 1437 AH
October 2015 CE

بسم الله الرحمن الرحيم

INTRODUCTION

Allah and His angels bless the Prophet. Believers, invoke blessings and peace on him.

(al-Aḥzāb 33: 56)

Allah lavishes His blessings on you (the Prophet Muḥammad) and His angels invoke blessings on you that He may lead you out of darkness into light.

(al-Aḥzāb 33: 43)

The above quoted Qur'ānic verses underscore the importance of reciting the Prophet Muḥammad's name and invoking blessings on him. This represents the highest felicity imaginable that Allah and His angels send blessings on him. Authentic Aḥādīth promise great rewards for reciting *ṣalawāt* (invoking blessings and peace on the Prophet Muḥammad). Equally noteworthy is the point that *ṣalawāt* forms part of the obligatory *ṣalāh* (prayer) offered five times a day by every Muslim.

The Qur'ān contains the following names, both personal and attributive, of the Prophet Muḥammad (peace be upon him):

- Muḥammad (*Āl ʿImrān* 3: 144)
- Aḥmad (*al-Ṣaff* 61: 6)
- ʿAbd Allāh (*al-Jinn* 72: 19)
- Al-Shāhid (*al-Aḥzāb* 33: 45)
- Al-Mubashshir (*al-Aḥzāb* 33: 35)
- Al-Ra'ūf (*al-Tawbah* 9: 128)
- Al-Muzzammil (*al-Muzzammil* 73: 1)
- Al-Hādī (*al-Raʿd* 13: 7)
- Al-Ḥaqq (*Yūnus* 10: 8)
- Al-Dāʿī ilā Allāh (*al-Aḥzāb* 33: 46)
- Al-Rasūl (*al-Nisā'* 4: 144)
- Al-Bashīr (*al-Baqarah* 2: 119)
- Al-Mudhakkir (*al-Ghāshiyah* 88: 21)
- Al-Raḥīm (*al-Tawbah* 9: 128)
- Al-Muddaththir (*al-Muddaththir* 74: 1)
- Yā Sīn (*Yā Sīn* 36: 1)
- Ṭā Hā (*Ṭā Hā* 20: 1)
- Sirāj Al-Munīr (*al-Aḥzāb* 33: 46)
- Khātim Al-Nabiyyīn (*al-Aḥzāb* 33: 40)
- Al-Burhān (*al-Nisā'* 4: 174)

- Al-Nadhīr (*al-Baqarah* 2: 119)
- Al-ʿAzīz (*al-Tawbah* 9: 128)
- Al-Amīn (*al-Takwīr* 81: 21)
- Al-Mundhir (*al-Raʿd* 13: 7)
- Raḥmat lil ʿĀlamīn (*al-Anbiyā'* 21: 107)
- Al-Nūr (*al-Mā'idah* 5: 15)
- Al-Shahīd (*al-Baqarah* 2: 143)
- Al-Nabī (*al-Anfāl* 8: 64)
- Al-ʿAbd (*al-Isrā'* 17: 1)

In view of the above, the Prophet's Companions (*Ṣaḥābah*) regarded it as their great privilege to record, elucidate, and transmit the Aḥādīth about the Prophet's names and attributes.

In the light of their study of the Qur'ān and Ḥadīth, Muslim scholars have enumerated hundreds of names and attributes of the Prophet which feature in Jalāl al-Dīn al-Suyūṭī's *Al-Bahjah Al-Bahiyyah fī Al-Asmā' Al-Nabwiyyah*, Muḥammad Ibn Yūsuf Ṣāliḥī Shāfiʿī's *Subul Al-Hudā* and Zurqānī's *Sharḥ Al-Mawāhib Al-Ludaniyyah*. Of these, his 99 names and attributes are widely known. Their study enables us not only to gain a better, clear picture of his excellent personality and laudable traits, it also helps us grasp and appreciate the all-embracing Islamic belief system and world view. Moreover, it instructs us how to lead life by emulating the role model embodied by the Prophet, for Allah proclaims: "*Surely there is a good example for you in the Messenger of Allah (the Prophet Muḥammad).*" (al-Aḥzāb 33:21) It thus inculcates into us love, respect, and regard for Allah's Final Messenger whom Allah "*sent down as mercy unto mankind.*" (al-Anbiyā' 21:107)

Islam is, no doubt, Allah-centred faith yet in its scheme of things, the Prophet Muḥammad (peace be upon him) occupies a central position. The Qur'ān declares:

> *Those who believe and do good deeds and believe in the revelations sent down to Muḥammad – for it is the truth from their Lord – He will remove from them their misdeeds and improve their condition.*
>
> (Muḥammad 47: 2)

In the above quoted passage, Allah assures Muslims forgiveness for their sins if they lead their life in accordance with the Divine message sent down to the

Prophet (peace be upon him). Our commitment to his message will bring us success in both this world and the next. He is part of the chain of Allah's Messengers who conveyed divine guidance to mankind. More remarkably, he stands out as the Final Messenger whose teachings are valid until the end of time. (al-Anʿām 6: 85–90 and al-Aḥzāb 33: 40) He belongs to the progeny of the Prophets Abraham, and Ishmael (peace be upon them). His appearance on the firmament of the seventh century Makkah signifies Allah's acceptance of the following fervent supplication made by the Prophets Abraham and Ishmael (peace be upon them):

> *Our Lord! Raise up for them (the children of Ishmael) a Messenger from among them who will recite to them Your revelations and will teach them the Book and Wisdom and will purify them (of sins and unbelief). Surely you alone are Almighty and All-Wise.*
>
> (al-Baqarah 2: 129)

It is on record that the Prophet (peace be upon him) accomplished the following missions in line with the import of the above verse: (a) conveying the meaning and message of the Qur'ān, (b) instructing everyone in Islamic faith and practices, and (c) facilitating redemption and salvation for people. His main assignment consisted in giving good news to believers, and warning unbelievers. Not only did he faithfully transmit the divine message, he also set the exemplary way of life. His distinguished life and conduct serve as the role model valid for all time and place. Little wonder then, that Allah elevated him to the highest station of praise and glory:

> *And We have exalted your fame*
>
> (Alam Nashraḥ 94: 4)

> *Your Lord will raise you to the rank of praise and glory*
>
> (al-Isrā' 17: 79)

Abiding by the Prophet's teachings represents obeying Allah, a point recurrently stated in the Qur'ān, Ḥadīh and Sunnah, his sayings and deeds respectively, are therefore of utmost importance in Islam and constitute the primary sources of Islamic faith.

Notwithstanding his many unique traits, the Prophet (peace be upon him) was a mortal human being and a servant of Allah chosen by Him to communicate and elucidate His message to mankind. He does not share any trait with divinity. It is all the more necessary to clarify this point in that some of his names mentioned in the Qur'ān itself and recounted in this book, are the same as those of Allah.

Throughout his career, the Prophet (peace be upon him) devoted himself heart and soul to preaching and practising the message of Islam and achieved amazing success in transforming the polytheistic, ignorant Arabs into champions of monotheism and knowledge. It is therefore not surprising to note the American author, Michael Hart acclaiming the Prophet (peace be upon him) as the most important person in history (*The 100: A Ranking of the Most Influential Persons in History*). Allah directs us to treat the Prophet (peace be upon him) with love and respect:

> *O Believers! Do not put yourself forward before Allah and His Messenger. But fear Allah. For Allah is All-Hearing, All-Knowing.*
>
> (al-Ḥujurāt 49: 1)

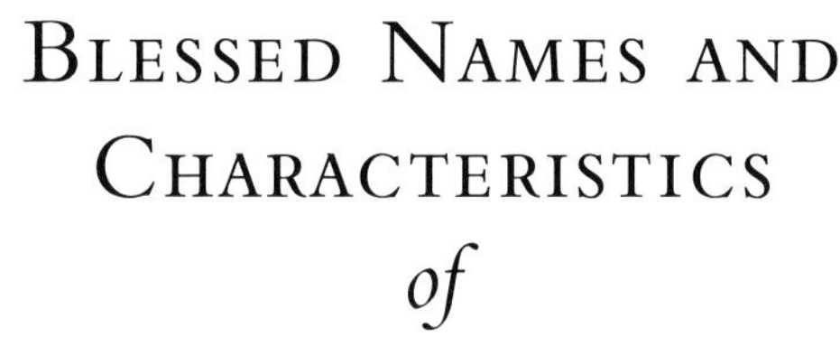

Blessed Names and Characteristics *of* The Prophet ﷺ Muḥammad

I

THE PRAISED ONE

THAT *Allah and angels send blessings upon the Prophet Muḥammad (peace be upon him)* (al-Aḥzāb 33: 56) points to his exalted status. The Qur'ān directs us: "*Believers, send blessings on him*" (al-Aḥzāb 33: 56). It also indicates that Allah praises him and blesses his mission. Allah has exalted his name and fame. His name figures along with Allah in the credal statement of Islam: لآ إِلَهَ إِلّا اللهُ مُحَمَّدٌ رَسُولُ اللهِ and in acts of devotional worship by billions of Muslims. This again shows how widely he is praised.

Muslims have immense love and respect for Him. Little wonder then that according to *The Columbia Encyclopaedia,* Muḥammad is the most common given name in the world. More than 150 million males presently bear this name. All this underscores Muslims' tremendous admiration for him. More significantly, it brings out the truth that he has been the most praised person in the annals of history.

We should recite *ṣalawāt* (benediction) as much as possible, particularly when his name is mentioned. This brings immense rewards from Allah.

2

أَحْمَدُ

HE WHO PRAISED ALLAH MUCH

THE Prophet Muḥammad (peace be upon him) holds the distinction of having praised Allah most by his acts of worship and by accomplishing the mission of Islam, which has enabled billions of people to recognize and worship and thus praise Allah.

Another remarkable point, according to the Qur'ān, is that the Prophet Jesus (peace be upon him) announced the Prophet's advent, saying that his name will be Aḥmad: "*O children of Israel, I am Allah's Messenger to you. I give you the glad tiding of a Messenger who shall come after me, his name being Aḥmad.*" (al-Ṣaff 61: 7).

From Sūrah al-Ṣaff 61: 6

The Prophet (peace be upon him) referred to it as one of his distinctions that Allah had named him Aḥmad (*Al-Tirmidhī, Al-Shamā'il Al-Muḥammadiyyah,* Bāb Mā Jā'a Fī Asmā' Rasūl Allāh, 356).

Like Muḥammad, Aḥmad happens to be a favourite name among Muslims. Out of their love and esteem

for the Prophet (peace be upon him) Muslims regard it as their great privilege to name their beloved babies after him.

3

الحَامِدُ

HE WHO PRAISED ALLAH

NOT only did the Prophet Muḥammad (peace be upon him) praise and glorify Allah profusely, he also did so in a befitting manner. In an extensive Ḥadīth it is related that all Messengers will direct the distressed people on the Day of Judgement to the Prophet Muḥammad (peace be upon him) for his intercession. He will prostrate before Allah and earnestly seek forgiveness for them. At that point too, he will invoke and praise Allah in the best manner.

The Prophet's Sunnah guides us how to invoke and praise Allah.

From Al-Bukhārī Kitāb al-Tawḥīd: 6,975

4

المَحْمُودُ

THE PRAISED ONE

From Sūrah al-Isrā' 17: 79

THAT the Prophet Muḥammad (peace be upon him) will win wide acclaim was foretold by the Qur'ān thus: "*Your Lord will soon raise you to an honoured position.*" (al-Isrā' 17: 79). Since then and up to our time he has held an eminent position, indicative of universal appreciation and admiration for him. In the Hereafter too, his glory will be enviable.

His piety, laudable morals and manners, and above all, his total devotion to Allah earned him such unrivalled fame and glory.

5

القَاسِمُ

HE WHO DISTRIBUTED ON ALLAH'S BEHALF

From *Al-Bukhārī* Kitāb al-Khums: 2,949

The Prophet (peace be upon him) benefitted humanity in many ways by sensitising them to faith, excellent morals and immense knowledge.

Furthermore, he distributed on Allah's behalf the 'spoils of war' and many assignments and opportunities to people which helped them much.

As a true, devout servant of Allah, he always credited Allah for all that he gave, declaring: "As to me, I only distribute. It is Allah alone Who grants all things."

The above Ḥadīth is yet another testimony to the Prophet's modesty and truthfulness. He was never after personal glory or grandeur; he attributed his success to Allah.

الفَاتِحُ

HE WHO OPENED THE DOORS

THE Qur'ān foretold the Prophet (peace be upon him) about his imminent victory: "*(O Prophet), surely We have granted you a clear victory.*" (al-Fatḥ 48: 1) It is not, therefore, surprising that he gained victory in all the battles, though he lacked the numbers and resources which his enemies had in plenty. More importantly, he won over the hearts and minds of millions through his excellent conduct and noble words.

Furthermore, he opened the doors for gaining Allah's mercy, for attaining spiritual development and for grasping and adhering to truth.

From Sūrah al-Fatḥ 48: 1

THE SEAL OF THE PROPHETS

AT the end of the long series of Allah's Messengers, the Prophet Muḥammad (peace be upon him) appeared, and this sealed the institution of Messengership and Prophethood. The Prophet (peace be upon him) made this point absolutely clear that no Messenger will ever appear after him.

From Sūrah al-Aḥzāb 33: 40

8

الحَاشِرُ

HE WHO WILL RESPOND TO ALLAH'S CALL IN THE HEREAFTER

WHILE describing his role, the Prophet (peace be upon him) clarified:

أَنَا الْحَاشِرُ الَّذِيْ يُحْشَرُ النَّاسُ عَلَىٰ قَدَمِي

(البخاری، کتاب المناقب)

I will be the first to rise on the Day of Resurrection and all will be gathered after me.

(Al-Bukhārī, *Kitāb al-Manāqib*)

It is one of the many distinctions enjoyed by the Prophet (peace be upon him), that he will be the first to be brought back to life on the Day of Judgement. He will be, thus, the first to respond to Allah's call for the grand assembly. All human beings will be assembled after him.

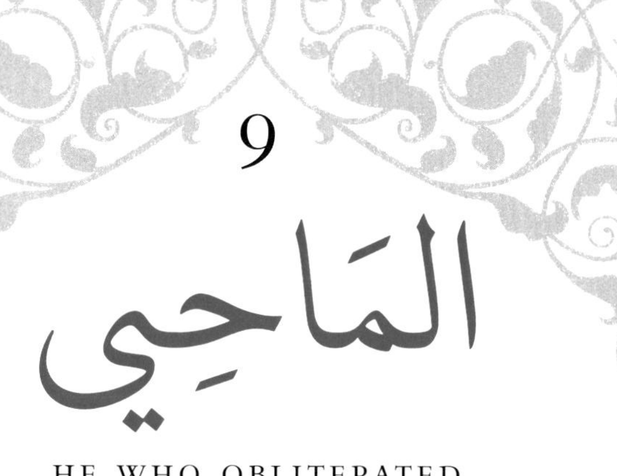

9

HE WHO OBLITERATED UNBELIEF

THE Qur'ān asked the Prophet (peace be upon him) to announce: "*Say (O Prophet): 'The truth has come and falsehood can neither originate nor recreate anything.'*" (Saba' 34: 49) The Qur'ānic assertion came true, thanks to the Prophet's and his Companions devotion to the cause of faith. In his own lifetime the Prophet (peace be upon him) witnessed the elimination of unbelief from the Arabian peninsula. At a later date, Islam spread to major parts of the world.

In keeping with the Prophet's mission we should promote faith and eliminate unbelief through preaching and persuasion.

From Sūrah Saba' 34: 49

THE CALLER TO TRUTH

From Sūrah al-Aḥzāb 33: 46

The Qur'ān introduces the Prophet Muḥammad (peace be upon him) as the "*one who calls people to Allah by His leave*". (al-Aḥzāb 33: 46) The Qur'ān further clarifies: "*And he who does not respond to the one who calls Allah will not be able to frustrate Him on earth. Nor will they have anyone to protect them from Allah. Such people are in manifest error.*" (al-Aḥqāf 46: 32)

Since his elevation to the august office of Allah's Messengership, until his last breath, the Prophet (peace be upon him) admirably performed his role of calling people to Allah's way. Through his word and deed and his impeccable conduct, he invited everyone to Islam and achieved remarkable success in this arduous task.

Our love and respect for him obliges us to continue his mission of calling people to Islam in the best manner.

11

السِّرَاجُ المُنِيرُ

THE ONE LIKE A BRIGHT SHINING LAMP

THE Qur'ān sets out the Prophet Muḥammad's assignment as follows: "*O Prophet, We have sent you forth as a witness, a bearer of good tidings, and a warner, and as one who calls people to Allah by His leave, as a bright, shining lamp.*" (al-Aḥzāb 33: 45–46) The metaphorical description of the Prophet (peace be upon him) as a bright, shining lamp brings out well his role. His message illuminates the whole world. It helped countless people to come out of the darkness of unbelief into the light of faith.

It is our duty to convey tactfully and effectively his message to everyone. This will make this world a better place to live in and will fetch us immense rewards from Allah.

From Sūrah al-Aḥzāb 33: 46

12

THE GUIDE

ACCORDING to a report, ʿAbdullāh ibn Umm Maktūm, a Companion, called on the Prophet (peace be upon him) and requested him to guide him. (Al-Tirmidhī, *Kitāb al-Tafsīr*: 3,331) Not only Ibn Umm Maktūm, but hundreds of thousands more were guided by the Prophet (peace be upon him). Moreover, millions continue to derive guidance from his life-giving and soul-enriching message. His illustrious life, actions and sayings serve as beacon lights. We should try our level best to draw upon this invaluable source of divine guidance.

From al-Tirmidhī Kitāb al-Tafsīr: 3,331

13

THE ILLUMINATING ONE

THE Qur'ān speaks figuratively of the Prophet (peace be upon him) as "*a bright shining lamp.*" (al-Aḥzāb 33: 46) Metaphorically, his advent illuminated the whole world steeped in the darkness of unbelief, idolatry and superstition. Likewise, he illumined the hearts and souls of those engaged in the quest for truth. His message enabled many to move into the light of faith, reason and tolerance.

Not only should we draw upon the light presented by him, we should also spread it far and wide.

From Sūrah  al-Aḥzāb 33: 46

14 THE BEARER OF GOOD NEWS

From Sūrah al-Baqarah 2: 119

THE following Qur'ānic verse uses and defines the expression, *Al-Bashīr* for the Prophet Muḥammad (peace be upon him). It also explains pithily the Islamic concept of a Prophet. These rules out any divinity of a Prophet: Tell them (O Muḥammad): "*I have no power to benefit or harm myself except as Allah may please. And had I knowledge of the unseen, I should have amassed all kinds of good, and no evil would have ever touched me. I am merely a warner, and the herald of glad tidings to those who have faith*". (al-Aʿrāf 7: 188)

The good tidings conveyed by the Prophet (peace be upon him) include: how to win Allah's pleasure; how to construct a happy, peaceful society; and how to attain self-development and self-purification. May Allah grant us the ability and strength to follow the same.

15

THE WARNER

THE Qur'ān directs the Prophet (peace be upon him) to apprise the Makkan unbelievers of his role: "*I am most certainly a plain warner.*" (al-Ḥijr 15: 89) In alerting mankind against the dire consequences of unbelief and the horrific punishment in Hell, the Prophet (peace be upon him) acted as a great benefactor of humanity.

In the face of the Prophet's graphic, unmistakable warnings about the misdeeds which incur Allah's displeasure, which will result in our loss and destruction in the Afterlife, we should be all the more particular about following his guidance.

From Sūrah al-Ḥijr 15: 89

HE WHO GUIDED

From Sūrah al-Ra'd 13:7

EQUIPPED with the divine revelation, the Prophet (peace be upon him) performed well his mandate of being the guide *par excellence* and his teachings continue to instruct us today. Embodied in him were all the qualities of a mentor: articulation, sincerity towards everyone and a kind, loving disposition.

We should draw as much as possible upon his eternally valid guidance and convey it to others as well.

17

THE MESSENGER

IN as many as 137 instances in the Qur'ān, Allah addresses the Prophet Muḥammad (peace be upon him) by his designation, "O Messenger". There is a slight distinction between a Prophet and a Messenger. A Messenger stands out above a Prophet, for he is granted the Holy Book. A Prophet carries out the same mission of spreading truth, though not endowed with an independent Scripture. Otherwise, for all practical purposes the two terms are almost the same.

What is more important is that we should emulate the Messenger's excellent example in our life.

From Sūrah al-Nisā' 4: 144

18

THE PROPHET

THE term "Al-Nabī" (the Prophet) is used twenty-five times in the Qur'ān. While addressing the Prophet (peace be upon him), and through him mankind of all time and place, Allah has conveyed a whole range of truths which are valuable for man to lead a life in accordance with His will.

In the Islamic scheme of things, a Prophet is a selected servant of Allah who invites people to truth, gives good news to those who embrace faith and warns those who reject it. He thus occupies a pivotal position in Allah-man relationship.

The Prophet Muḥammad, (peace be upon him) being the Last Prophet, holds a more exalted position and must be obeyed by all of us.

From Sūrah  al-Anfāl 8: 64

ṬĀ HĀ

Like *Ṭā Sīn,* it also comprises the abbreviated letters of the Qur'ān. This marks the opening of the Qur'ānic Sūrah *Ṭā Hā*. Qāḍī ʿIyāḍ, Ṣālihī, Tamīmī and Bayhaqī maintain that *Ṭā Hā* represents one of the names of the Prophet Muḥammad (peace be upon him). On reading Sūrah *Ṭā Hā,* in the opening verse together with the next verse, it appears that it is some form of address employed for the Prophet (peace be upon him).

From Sūrah Ṭā Hā 20: 1

YĀ SĪN

THIS abbreviated formula at the beginning of the Qur'ānic Sūrah *Yā Sīn* is construed by some Qur'ān scholars as one of the names of the Prophet Muḥammad (peace be upon him). Since no definite meaning of the abbreviated letters of the Qur'ān is on record, it is hard to say what Sūrah *Yā Sīn* exactly means. However, since this expression is immediately followed in the next verse addressing the Prophet (peace be upon him), it appears that it is a form of address used by Allah for the Prophet (peace be upon him).

Such eminent Qur'ān scholars as ʿAbdullāh ibn ʿAbbās, Ibn Masʿūd and Bayhaqī, hold that *Yā Sīn* stands for the Prophet (peace be upon him). This interpretation, however, does not represent the consensus view.

21

THE ENWRAPPED ONE

In the early days of his Prophetic mission, the Prophet (peace be upon him) learnt about the Makkan unbelievers' council planning their tirade against him. As he lay, feeling bad about their apathy and opposition to truth, he received this comforting, inspiring piece of revelation from Allah: "*O you the enwrapped one! Stand up in prayer by night, all but a small part of it; half of it; or reduce it a little; or add to it a little; and recite the Qur'ān slowly and distinctly.*" (al-Muzzammil 73: 1–4)

The lesson for us from the above is to engage in prayer and the Qur'ān recitation when in distress. This will revive our spirit and enable us to take on any adversity.

22

المُدَّثِّرُ

THE ONE ENVELOPED IN THE CLOAK

From Sūrah al-Muddaththir 74: 1

This is another Qur'ānic appellation for the Prophet (peace be upon him), referring to his dress. More importantly, this form of address to him asks him to preach Islam publicly, though in an extremely hostile setting: "*O you enveloped in your cloak! Arise and warn, and magnify the glory of your Lord.*" (al-Muddaththir 74: 1–3)

We are, thus, directed to derive inspiration and strength from the Word of God in unfavourable circumstances. The Prophet's illustrious example is before us: how successfully he preached Islam in and around Makkah amid severe opposition and persecution.

23

الشَّفِيعُ

HE WHO WILL INTERCEDE

The Prophet (peace be upon him) told about this distinction of his that Allah will allow him to intercede on the Day of Judgement.

For availing ourselves of this, we should make it a point to recite *ṣalawāt* as many times as possible for the Prophet (peace be upon him).

From Sūrah  Ṭā Hā 20: 109

FRIEND OF ALLAH

In one Ḥadīth report the Prophet's status as Allah's friend is spelled out. This points to the Prophet's exalted status.

A friend in the context of Allah signifies someone close to Him in view of his impeccable character and conduct. Allah graciously conferred this coveted appellation on the Prophets Abraham and Muḥammad (peace be upon them).

From Sharḥ Sunan al-Nasā'ī 3, 406

25

كَلِيمُ اللّٰهِ

THE ONE TO WHOM ALLAH SPOKE

ABOUT the Messengers of Allah, the Qur'ān informs: "*Allah exalted some of them above the others. Among them are such as were spoken to by Allah Himself, and some He exalted in other respects*". (al-Baqarah 2: 253) According to Ḥadīth reports about the Prophet's ascension (*miʿrāj*), Allah spoke to him and gave instructions regarding the obligatory prayer.

The Prophet Muḥammad (peace be upon him), thus, shares this honour with the Prophet Moses (peace be upon him), who is also known by the title *Kalīm Allāh,* for Allah's conversation with him is recorded in the Qur'ān.

From Sūrah  al-Baqarah 2: 253

THE BELOVED PROPHET OF ALLAH

From al-Tirmidhī  Abwāb al-Manāqib: 3,616

ACCORDING to ʿAbdullāh ibn ʿAbbās, the Prophet (peace be upon him) informed: "I am the beloved Prophet of Allah, and I say this without any pride. And on the Day of Judgement I will carry the banner of His praise. Again, I say this without any pride." (Al-Tirmidhī, *Abwāb al-Manāqib*: 3,616)

Allah's love enabled the Prophet (peace be upon him) to devote himself all the more to truth, faith and good. Accordingly, he grew into a paragon of virtues.

THE CHOSEN ONE

THE Prophet Muḥammad (peace be upon him) is the chosen one in view of his following major distinctions:

- Being the Final Messenger of Allah;
- Being the mercy unto the worlds;
- Being the intercessor by Allah's leave on the Day of Judgement;
- Being the first to rise from his grave and the first to enter Paradise;
- Being the leader of all Messengers of Allah;
- Being foretold in all the Scriptures.

As members of his community, it is our responsibility to spread his message.

From Sūrah  al-Ḥajj 22: 75

المُرْتَضَىٰ

THE PREFERRED ONE

From Sūrah al-Jinn 72: 26–27

The Qur'ān states that Allah chooses whom He wills as His Messenger. The Prophet Muḥammad (peace be upon him), a devout person who was in the quest for truth, was selected by Allah for this august office. Though he was an orphan and was vulnerable, Allah chose him for his piety and sincerity. Soon after his appointment to his Messengership, he proved his mettle as Islam was firmly established in Arabia, notwithstanding stiff opposition, persecution and exile.

The Prophet's career, studded with his exceptional perseverance, courage and sincerity of purpose, is there for us to emulate. We should likewise strive for upholding and strengthening Islam in both our personal and collective life.

29

المُجْتَبَى

THE SELECT ONE

ALLAH tells us that He selects whom He wills as His Messenger. (Āl 'Imrān 3: 89) The Prophet (peace be upon him) rose to the occasion and accomplished the tasks assigned to him.

Let us take stock of our conduct in order to assess how true we are to the mission assigned to us by Allah and His Messenger.

From Sūrah Āl 'Imrān 3: 179

30

THE HELPER

From Sūrah al-Anfāl 8: 72

FIRST and foremost, the Prophet Muḥammad (peace be upon him) helped, rather, strengthened the cause of true faith by preaching it vigorously and effectively. It was his heroic mission which culminated in establishing Islam far and wide in his lifetime and at a later date. Furthermore, he salvaged mankind by showing the way to eternal success and by warning against eternal perdition. He drove many from darkness into the light of divine guidance and their eventual deliverance.

On the sociocultural level, he gave a new lease of life to the weak, the underprivileged and the oppressed. His egalitarian message ushered in an era of freedom for many deprived sections of society. In his personal capacity too, he helped those in need and alleviated their suffering.

May Allah enable us to follow in his footsteps which will lead to improving the lot of fellow human beings.

31

HE WHO WAS HELPED

ALLAH helped the Prophet Muḥammad (peace be upon him) on numerous occasions in discharging his duty as His Messenger and in protecting him. Here is one example, featuring in the Qur'ān: "*Allah surely helped him when the unbelievers drove him out of his home and he was but one of the two when they were in the cave …*" (al-Tawbah 9: 40) Reference is to the Prophet's emigration to Madinah along with his Companion, Abū Bakr, when they hid inside a cave from the murderous, Makkan unbelievers. Allah saved him in a miraculous fashion.

Like him, we should seek help from Allah, as only He can help us.

From Sūrah al-Tawbah 9: 40

القَائِمُ

HE WHO ROSE TO CALL TO ISLAM

From Sūrah al-Jinn 72: 19

THE Prophet Muḥammad's steadfast role in making the call to Islam is commended at several places in the Qur'ān (al-Jinn 72: 19, al-Rūm 30: 30, al-Muzzammil 73:2 and al-Muddaththir 74: 2). It was his consistent striving in the cause of faith which eventually helped establish Islam in Arabia and beyond. The odds against his mission were formidable. He faced rejection, persecution, exile, torture, slander and even wars. However, aided by Allah and supported by his devout, spirited Companions he achieved a historic success in his mission.

The Prophet's mission should serve as a source of strength and inspiration. It should help us practise and preach our faith in any adverse circumstances we may face.

HE WHO GUARDED

The Prophet (peace be upon him) guarded the Divine revelation as he faithfully conveyed it to his scribes and Companions. As a result, the Qur'ān is preserved to this day in its pristine purity. Moreover, his teaching and preaching enabled many to guard their faith, their heart and their body against Satan's promptings.

We stand indebted to the Prophet (peace be upon him) for his safeguarding us against evil, especially polytheism.

From Zurqānī Sharḥ al-Mawāhib al-Laddunīyah 4,182

34

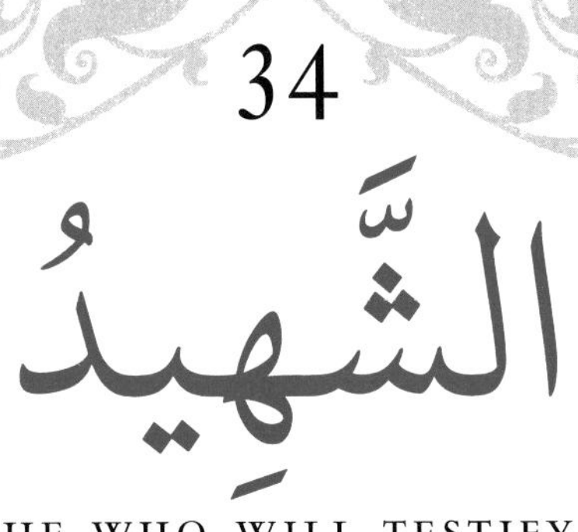

HE WHO WILL TESTIFY

From Sūrah al-Baqarah 2: 143

ALLAH's scheme regarding His Messengers and believers is as follows: "*We appointed you (O Believers) to be the community of the middle way so that you might be witnesses to all mankind and the Messenger might be a witness to you.*" (al-Baqarah 2: 143)

On the Day of Judgement, the Prophet Muḥammad (peace be upon him) will testify that he had conveyed Allah's message to mankind through his word and deed. More importantly, we will be asked to testify that through our conduct we had exemplified what Islam is. This is an important responsibility about which we should be careful.

Muslims are defined here as, "the community of the middle way", i.e. those who avoid extremes and follow a way marked by balance and justice. Let us strive to fulfil this role assigned to us by Allah.

35

THE JUST ONE

PIETY, justice and honesty were the outstanding traits of the Prophet's character. While performing admirably his role as the head and leader of the Muslim community he always observed the dictates of justice. His fairness was acknowledged even by his enemies. Even in his pre-Prophetic days, he was entrusted with arbitration because everyone knew that his decision would be based wholly on justice.

All along he urged Muslims to stand for justice. Early Muslim victors were welcomed by their non-Muslim subjects, once again, owing to their adherence to justice.

May Allah grant us the ability and strength to rise to the ideals of justice and fairness.

From Sūrah al-Shūrā 42: 15

THE JUDGE

APART from preaching truth, Allah entrusted the Prophet Muḥammad (peace be upon him) with the duty of dispensing justice and pronouncing judgements as part of his Prophetic role. The Qur'ān directed him: "*(O Messenger), We have revealed to you this Book with truth so that you may judge between people in accordance with what Allah has shown you.*" (al-Nisā' 4: 105). The same directives to him appear in verses 48 and 49 of Sūrah al-Mā'idah.

From Sūrah al-Nisā' 4: 105

Being the Messenger of Allah, he had the authority to decide matters in line with divine law. He discharged this duty, like his other assignments, admirably. We are obliged to abide by his judgements.

37

النُّورُ

THE LIGHT

THE Qur'ān introduces the Prophet Muḥammad (peace be upon him) thus: "*O People of the Book! Now Our Messenger has come to you; he makes clear to you many things of the Book which you used to conceal, and also passes over many things. There has now come to you a light from Allah, and a clear Book*". (al-Mā'idah 5: 15) Many Qur'ān scholars, for example; 'Abdullāh ibn 'Abbās, Khāzin, Bayḍāwī, Nasafī, Qurṭubī and Shawkānī, take this "light" to mean the Prophet (peace be upon him). For he enlightened everyone about truth. The use of the metaphor of light for him is very apt. For in the light of his word and deed we can easily see what pleases Allah and what does not.

From Sūrah al-Mā'idah 5: 15

38

THE DIVINE ARGUMENT

From Sūrah al-Nisā' 4: 145

THE Qur'ān speaks of Messengers as Allah's arguments. For Allah did not want unbelievers to have any basis for pleading their ignorance of the true faith. In the face of the series of Messengers sent down in various eras, in almost all parts of the world, the unbelievers could not say that no arrangement had been made by Allah to guide them to the truth.

The miracles granted by Allah to His Messengers represent another divine argument. For those unbelievers who witnessed divine miracles cannot offer any plausible reason for their persistence in unbelief and for their rejection of truth.

In sum, Allah has sent many arguments, as for example, Messengers, books and miracles, which vindicate divine truth.

39

ALLAH'S CLINCHING ARGUMENT

THE Qur'ān proclaims: "*O people! A proof has come to you from your Lord, and We have sent down to you a clear light.*"(al-Nisā' 4: 174). Apart from himself being the divine proof, the Prophet (peace be upon him) brought many evident signs which underscore Allah's Oneness and creative wonders. The Qur'ān and the Prophet's unblemished life stand out as the two prominent signs. That the Prophet's wife, close family members and friends were the first to accept his claim to be Allah's Messenger, also represents an evident sign of the truth embodied by him.

The Prophet's role model being a self evident sign of Allah should be emulated by us as much as possible.

From Sūrah al-Nisā' 4: 174

FATHER OF THE TRUE BELIEVERS

From Sūrah al-Aḥzāb 33: 6

THE Qur'ān states that the Prophet Muḥammad (peace be upon him) was closer to his Companions than their own selves (al-Aḥzāb 33: 6). Like a good father, he always felt concerned for their welfare, met their needs and strove for their moral and spiritual development. He sacrificed his valuable time, energy and resources for the better prospects of his Companions.

41

THE STRONG ONE

Both literally and metaphorically the Prophet Muḥammad (peace be upon him) stands out as someone strong. As a highly influential figure, he changed lives, at individual and collective levels, and also the course of history. Physically, he was a strong, energetic person. Jābir, a Companion, recounts with awe that as part of the preparation for the Battle of Confederates, when Muslims in Madinah were engaged in digging a trench for self-defence, he broke boulders into pieces with a single blow which others could not. As to the strength of his character and conduct, let us remember that for hundreds of years and for millions of people he has been the source of inspiration and strength.

From al-Bukhārī Kitāb al-Maghāzī: 3,875

42

THE COUNSELLOR

ALLAH mentions in the Qur'ān that He directed the Prophet (peace be upon him) to render good counsel (al-Ghāshiyah 88: 21). That the Prophet's name is mentioned along with Allah's in *adhān* and *takbīr* (call to Prayer), *shahādah* (the credal statement of Islam), Friday sermon and *ṣalawāt* which is recited as part of prayer, it is little wonder that the Qur'ān speaks of him as *the* role model (al-Aḥzāb 33: 21). It is in our own interest to earnestly emulate his example.

From Sūrah al-Ghāshiyah 88: 21

43

THE ADMONISHER

THE Qur'ān advises the Prophet (peace be upon him) to counsel people so that they may stand up for the cause of truth (Sabā' 34: 45). Accordingly, throughout his Prophetic career he urged people to embrace and adhere to truth. His counseling paid rich dividends. In his own lifetime, most of Arabia greeted his message.

It is now obligatory on us to keep advising people to work for the cause of truth.

From Sūrah  Saba' 34: 45

44

THE TRUSTWORTHY

In recognition of the Prophet's integrity and fair dealings, which adorned even his pre-Prophetic life of forty years in Makkah, the unbelieving Makkans had bestowed upon him the complimentary title, *al-Amīn* (the trustworthy). They were, however, so blind in their commitment to their ancestral faith and idols that they refused to believe in the message of truth presented by him.

The Prophet (peace be upon him) placed much premium on the virtue of trustworthiness, as is recorded in this Ḥadīth:

وَأَنَا أَمِيْنُ مَنْ فِي السَّمَاءِ، يَأْتِيْنِي خَبَرُ السَّمَاءِ صَبَاحاً وَمَسَاءً

(البخاري ، كتاب المغازي)

I am trustworthy also regarding the high above, for I receive these tidings every morning and evening.

(Al-Bukhārī, *Kitāb al-Maghāzī*)

45

الصَّادِقُ

THE TRUTHFUL ONE

THE Qur'ān portrays the Prophet (peace be upon him) thus: "*He who brought the truth and those who confirmed it as true, such are the pious ones.*" (al-Zumar 39: 33) Even in his pre-Prophetic life, he stood out above others as someone true to his word. Accordingly, the Makkan unbelievers called him *al-Ṣādiq* (the truthful one). The same trait of his truthfulness marked his Prophetic career as he faithfully transmitted the divine revelation sent to him. That Allah reposed trust in him is the most weighty proof of his truthfulness.

From Sūrah al-Zumar 39: 33

46

ٱلْمُصَدِّقُ

HE WHO CONFIRMED

From Sūrah Āl ʿImrān 3: 8

As part of his Prophetic assignment, the Prophet Muḥammad (peace be upon him) confirmed the earlier Messengers and Scriptures of Allah. For all of them contained and preached the same truth which Allah had conveyed to him as well. However, since the earlier Scriptures had been corrupted and the teachings of Messengers had been disregarded, Allah sent him to renew and revive the message of truth.

Being members of his community it is now our duty to confirm and spread his message.

47

النَّاطِقُ بِالحَقِّ

HE WHO SPOKE TRUTH

THE Qur'ān informs that the Prophet Muḥammad (peace be upon him) did not speak out of his desire. Rather, he always spoke truth. All of his words and actions were directed at instructing people how to draw closer to Allah.

As part of his community, we should be very particular about all what we say. Our words should not smack of anything false or unlawful. We should do and say only what is right and good.

From Sūrah al-Najm 53: 3

48

الصَّاحِبُ

THE COMPANION

From Sūrah al-Najm 53: 2

THIS honorific title in Arabic is used for a familiar figure. The Qur'ān employs it at places for the Prophet Muḥammad (peace be upon him) to impress upon the Makkan unbelievers the fact that the Prophet (peace be upon him) is no stranger to them. He is one of them, born and brought up among them and has spent forty years of his pre-Prophetic life before their eyes. All along they regarded him as a truthful and trustworthy person. Had he been an ambitious person with lust for power, they would have been the first to note it. They should, therefore, reconsider their stance of rejecting outright his call to truth.

Needless to add, among his Companions the Prophet (peace be upon him) commanded tremendous respect in view of his unblemished conduct and exemplary character.

49

A MEMBER OF THE QURAYSH TRIBE

Reference is to his descent from the Quraysh tribe and Banū Hāshim's family. The Quraysh were the noblest tribe of Arabia. They were the custodians of the house of Allah, Kaʿbah. The Prophet's ancestor Hāshim was an influential member of this tribe. The above Ḥadīth, therefore, speaks of him as a *Qurashī* and *Hāshimī*, alluding to his ancestral nobility.

Al-Bāb al-Awwal: 45

From Ibn Mājah

50

الأُمِّيُّ

THE UNLETTERED ONE

From Sūrah al-Aʿrāf 7: 115

THE divine origin of the Prophet's mission is supported also by the fact that he was an unlettered person who did not have access to any source of knowledge in his pre-Prophetic life. The Qur'ān cites the same as proof for the genuineness of his claim. "*(O Prophet), you did not recite any book before. Nor did you write it down with your hand; for then the false ones could have a cause for doubt.*" (al-ʿAnkabūt 29: 48)

Amazingly enough, this unlettered person turned out to be the greatest teacher of mankind for all time. Not only the early Muslims, even today millions derive guidance from Ḥadīth and Sunnah, which represent his sayings and actions, respectively.

HE WHO WAS DEEPLY CONCERNED

ON the Prophet Muḥammad's concern for fellow human beings, the following Qur'ānic passage is instructive: "*There has come to you a Messenger of Allah from among yourselves, who is distressed by the losses you sustain*', who *is ardently desirous of your welfare*". (al-Tawbah 9: 128) He felt very anxious about the fate of fellow Makkans and Arabs, for he knew full well that their rejection of true faith will bring about their eternal perdition. He, therefore, did all that he could in bringing everyone to the light of faith.

We should be concerned about unbelievers and should act sincerely and tactfully towards drawing them closer to true faith.

From Sūrah al-Tawbah 9: 128

Although it is a divine name, the Qur'ān mentions it as the Prophet Muḥammad's name as well.

52

الرَّؤُوف

THE TENDER ONE

THE Prophet's overflowing love and affection for believers is recorded, thus, in the Qur'ān: "*There has come to you a Messenger of Allah from among yourselves, who is distressed by the losses you sustain, who is ardently desirous of your welfare and is tender and merciful to those that believe.*" (al-Tawbah 9: 128)

This trait of his was an essential part of his excellent conduct. For Allah had sent him down as an exemplar. His affection for the weak and children is most instructive for us.

From Sūrah al-Tawbah 9: 128

Although it is a divine name, the Qur'ān mentions it as the Prophet Muḥammad's name as well.

53

الرَّحِيمُ

THE MERCIFUL ONE

THE Qur'ān states that the Prophet (peace be upon him) was merciful to believers. (al-Tawbah 9: 128) For inculcating kindness into people, he used to tell them: "He who does not show mercy will not get any mercy from Allah" (Al-Bukhārī, 5,997).

Being so merciful, he even pardoned the killer of his beloved uncle, Ḥamzah. Moreover, prompted by the same, he ensured that the weak, the poor, women and orphans are treated kindly and get their due.

From Sūrah al-Tawbah 9: 128

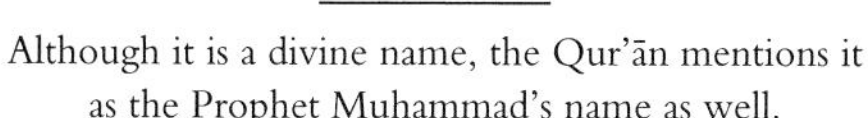

Although it is a divine name, the Qur'ān mentions it as the Prophet Muḥammad's name as well.

THE ORPHAN

From Sūrah al-Ḍuḥā 93: 6

WHILE recounting Allah's special favours to the Prophet Muḥammad (peace be upon him), the Qur'ān mentions that though he was an orphan, Allah raised him to great heights. Allah instilled abundant love for him in the hearts of his patrons – his grandfather, ʿAbd al-Muṭṭalib, and later his uncle, Abū Ṭālib. They loved him so dearly that he did not miss much his deceased father. Furthermore, by dint of his excellent conduct and accomplishments, he endeared himself to millions, both in his lifetime and at a later day. Notwithstanding his modest credentials as an orphan, he rose to be the most influential person in world history.

55

الغنيّ

HE WHO WAS ENRICHED BY ALLAH

AT places the Qur'ān states that out of His grace Allah enriched the Prophet Muḥammad (peace be upon him). This is most graphically recounted in Sūrah al-Ḍuḥā thus; "*did He not find you in want, and then enriched you?*" Reference is to enriching him in every sense of the term – intellectually, physically, morally and spiritually.

We should earnestly pray to Allah for his special favour of reinforcing us.

From Sūrah al-Tawbah 9: 74

Although it is a divine name, the Qur'ān mentions it as the Prophet Muḥammad's name as well.

56

THE GENEROUS ONE

THE Prophet Muḥammad (peace be upon him) set an example of donating all that he had in Allah's way. Never did he turn away anyone who asked him for help. Whenever he received some money or gift, he distributed these while sitting in his mosque. He did not return home without disposing all that he had. According to ʿAbdullāh ibn ʿAbbās: "During Ramaḍān he turned more generous, as swift as wind." (Al-Bukhārī, *Kitāb Bad' al-Waḥy*: 6)

We should try to emulate him on this particular count by acting generously towards all those around us.

Although it is a divine name, the Qur'ān mentions it as the Prophet Muḥammad's name as well.

57

الفَتَّاحُ

HE WHO RESOLVED DISPUTES

In his capacity as the head of the Islamic state and as the legislator authorized by Allah, the Prophet (peace be upon him) used to pronounce judgements on a range of issues. In resolving disputes, he always dispensed justice with compassion and leniency, encouraging mutual understanding, arbitration and amicable solution to disputes which could otherwise disfigure the social fabric.

Even in his pre-Prophetic days he was entrusted with settling disputes in view of his integrity and honesty.

We should make it a point to follow this feature of the Prophet's glorious example.

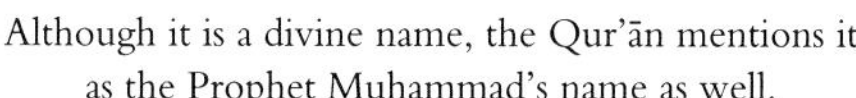

Although it is a divine name, the Qur'ān mentions it as the Prophet Muḥammad's name as well.

58

THE CUSTODIAN

From al-Suyūṭī Al-Riyāḍ al-Anīqah: 231

PROPHET Muḥammad (peace be upon him) was the custodian of the divine revelation brought to him by the Archangel, Gabriel. His impeccable integrity was acclaimed, even in his pre-Prophetic days, by friends and foes alike. The Makkans used to entrust their valuables to his custody, and as head of the Islamic community he was in charge of the public treasury. More importantly, people confided in him and sought his valuable, sincere advice on a variety of issues, including their personal problems.

This name of his brings into sharper light his unblemished character and conduct.

59

الطَّيِّبُ

THE PURE ONE

THE Prophet Muḥammad (peace be upon him) personified purity – of body, thought and soul. His Companions report that his body exuded such fragrance which captivated them. His mind was the seat of noble ideas and was enriched immensely by revelation. His spirit attained the heights of purity as he gained proximity with Allah.

All this should prompt us also to strive for attaining the purity of both mind and heart.

From Muslim Kitāb al-Faḍā'il: 2,330

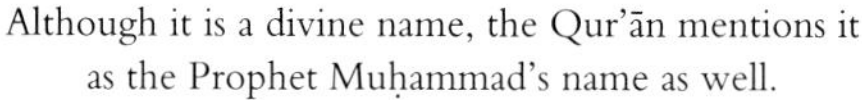

Although it is a divine name, the Qur'ān mentions it as the Prophet Muḥammad's name as well.

60

الطَّاهِرُ

THE PURE ONE

From Sūrah al-Aḥzāb 33: 33

THE Qur'ān declares that Allah condoned the Prophet's lapses. (al-Fatḥ 48: 2) His purity is, thus, well established. In the divine scheme of things, a Messenger is a sinless person under Allah's constant care and protection. The Qur'ān mentions that in his capacity as Allah's Messenger, the Prophet (peace be upon him) used to cleanse the believers, ensuring their growth in righteousness (al-Tawbah 9: 103). Ḥadīth reports record the sinning people approaching him, with a request to cleanse them (Dārimī, *Al-Sunan,* 2,329).

61

HE WHO PURGES

One of the main concerns of the Prophet Muḥammad (peace be upon him) throughout his blessed mission was to purge people of polytheism and unbelief. It was an arduous task, for his immediate addressees, the unbelieving Arabs of and around Makkah, had been steeped in polytheism for generations. Any deviation from their ancestral faith sounded outrageous to them. Blind to truth, they plainly refused to listen to him or to see reason. Yet, by means of his dedication, excellent conduct, and above all, divine help, he accomplished the heroic task of winning them over to Islam.

When early Muslims committed some lapse, they immediately turned to the Prophet (peace be upon him), imploring him to purge them of their misconduct. The Qur'ān had directed him to perform this role: "*(O Prophet), take charity out of their wealth and cleanse them and bring about their righteous growth, and pray for them.*" (al-Tawbah 9: 103)

From Sūrah al-Tawbah 9: 103

THE SPEAKER AMONG THE PROPHETS

THE Prophet Muḥammad (peace be upon him) excelled as an eloquent speaker. His sayings, recorded in the Ḥadīth collections, bear out his literary and rhetorical prowess. It is not, therefore, surprising to come across reports that in the grand assembly on the Day of Judgement when all, including other Prophets, will be silent, only the Prophet Muḥammad (peace be upon him) will speak before Allah.

The above underscores also the Prophet's exalted status among Prophets.

THE ELOQUENT ONE

THE Prophet Muḥammad (peace be upon him) is on record, saying: "I have been granted by Allah the most pithy words". The above is borne out by some of his terse, eloquent sayings which feature in Ḥadīth collections. Allah granted him the faculty of articulating his views effectively and energetically. His brilliant presentation skill was one of the factors contributing to his phenomenal success.

May Allah enable us to express ourselves clearly, especially in the cause of faith.

From Sūrah al-Nisā' 4: 63

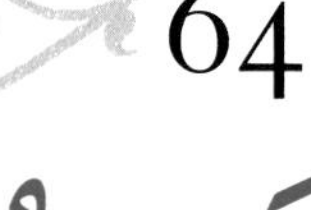

THE LEADER

From Sūrah al-Aʿrāf 7:158

APART from being the beloved and undisputed leader of the Muslim community throughout his blessed life, the Prophet (peace be upon him) will enjoy the same distinction on the Day of Judgement.

According to Abū Hurayrah, the Prophet (peace be upon him) informed: "I will be the leader of all communities on the Day of Judgement" (Al-Bukhārī, *Kitāb al-Anbiyā'*, 3,162).

While keeping in mind his privileged position in the Hereafter, we should be all the more particular about obeying him in life and glorifying him through reciting *ṣalawāt*.

65

HE WHO PURIFIES

As part of his Prophetic assignment the Prophet Muḥammad (peace be upon him) performed also the role of a spiritual master and mentor. His teachings transformed people's heart and mind. Those given to idolatry turned overnight into devout believers under the influence of his life-giving message. As the leader of the community, he ensured the spiritual and moral development of believers. Furthermore, he advised them sincerely on moral and spiritual matters.

We should be particular about our own moral and spiritual training and of those under our care.

From Sūrah Āl ʿImrān 3: 164

66

إِمَامُ الْمُتَّقِينَ

LEADER OF THE PIOUS ONES

From Sūrah al-Nūr 24: 52

THE Qur'ān promises that those who obey and fear Allah will achieve eternal success. As the Prophet Muḥammad (peace be upon him) stood out above all on both counts, the appellation of being the foremost among the pious befits only him. His noble life, recorded meticulously in all its detail, illustrates the high degree of his God-consciousness and piety.

We should always have his standard as the model to follow. For this alone, guarantees our success and happiness.

HE WHO GAVE SOLACE

As the community head and spiritual master, the Prophet (peace be upon him) was a source of moral, spiritual and emotional strength and inspiration for Muslims. His sermons and moral aphorisms provided them with much solace. Likewise, he comforted and consoled them when they were in distress, whether individual or collective. At times, he instructed them as to what may cure them from certain ailments. However, this was not his primary role as the Messenger of Allah. He was there for ensuring the moral and spiritual development of believers, and he accomplished this task remarkably.

From Sūrah al-Tawbah 9: 103

68

المُتَوَسِّطُ

HE WHO FOLLOWED THE MIDDLE PATH

From Sūrah al-Baqarah 2: 143

ALLAH brands the Muslim community as: "*the community of the middle way.*" (al-Baqarah 2: 143) What it signifies is balance, moderation and avoiding extremism. As the head of the Muslim community, the Prophet (peace be upon him) displayed these traits at their best. His actions and rulings are characterized by a strong note of moderation. More importantly, he always opted for a compassionate, lenient ruling, if possible. Notwithstanding his clemency, he never made any adjustment or bargaining on articles of faith. Polytheism, in all its forms, was totally unacceptable to him.

While we should be friendly towards others, we should not let any un-Islamic belief or act creep into our mind and heart.

69

HE WHO EXCELLED IN DOING GOOD

THE Qur'ān speaks highly of such believers who vie with and excel over others in doing good (Fāṭir 35: 32, al-Tawbah 9: 100, al-Mu'minūn 23: 61 and al-Wāqiʿah 56: 10). Of all the believers, the Prophet (peace be upon him) was the first and foremost in worshipping and serving Allah and in all acts of virtue. Accordingly, he serves as the role model for all Muslims.

In keeping with this bright example, we should strive to compete with others in doing good.

From Sūrah al-Fatḥ 48: 2

70

المُقْتَصِدُ

HE WHO FOLLOWED THE MIDDLE WAY

From Sūrah Fāṭir 35: 32

ISLAM being the natural way, prescribed by Allah Who is the Creator of man, asks man to follow the middle path, avoiding extremes. This signifies moderation and balance. The Prophet Muḥammad (peace be upon him) exemplified this at its best. His whole life represents a moderate, midway course. The Qur'ān designates Muslims as the community of "*the middle way.*" (al-Baqarah 2: 143)

The above name means that the Prophet (peace be upon him) followed and preached the path of justice and equity and maintained his relationship with others, based on piety and justice.

As members of his *ummah*, we should adhere to moderation, especially in our time when Islam is generally maligned as the faith of fanatics, in the wake of the outrageous misdeeds of some mindless, misguided persons.

71

THE GUIDED ONE

In Sūrah Al-Fatḥ, Allah promises the Prophet Muḥammad (peace be upon him) that He will guide him to the straight way. This promise came true on a massive scale. For he guided many in his lifetime and his teachings continue to draw millions to the path of truth.

Significantly enough, he used to make this supplication: "O Lord, adorn us with the splendour of faith and make us the leader of the guided ones" (*Aḥmad*: 4,264).

In line with the Prophet's excellent practice we should keep praying to Allah for increasing our faith and for enabling us to adhere to Allah's guidance.

From Sūrah al-Fatḥ 48: 2

72

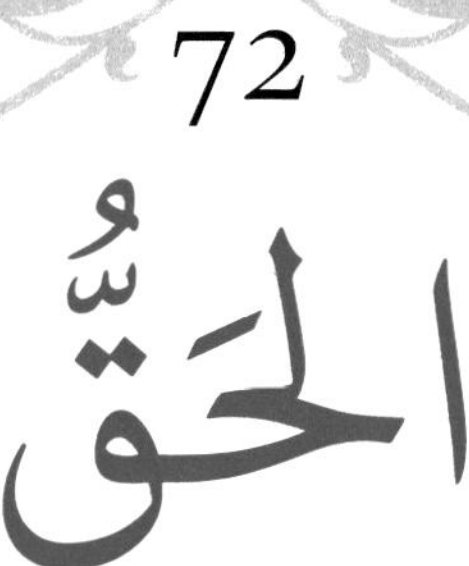

THE TRUTH

As the Prophet Muḥammad (peace be upon him) brought the Qur'ān which represents truth, he too is identified as truth in the Qur'ān. His illustrious life and his life-ennobling teachings embody truth. His devotion to truth was such that even his detractors acknowledged it, although they refused to accept Islam because of their clinging to the pagan ways of their ancestors.

From Sūrah Yūnus 10:8

THE MANIFEST ONE

THE Qur'ān announces the advent of the manifest Messenger, the Prophet Muḥammad (peace be upon him) (al-Dukhān 44: 13).

He is designated so in view of these two reasons:

(i) His truthfulness and excellent character and conduct were known to the people to whom he called to accept Islam.

(ii) He clearly explained Allah's commands and guidance, as contained in the Qur'ān. This culminated in the codification of Islamic law (*sharīʿah*) and the emergence of the distinct Muslim community.

From Sūrah  al-Ḥijr 15: 89

74

THE FIRST ONE

ACCORDING to the Ḥadīth related by Qatādah, the Prophet Muḥammad (peace be upon him) is the first one on these two counts:

(i) Of all of Allah's Messengers, his soul was created first, though he was sent as the last one.

(ii) On the Day of Resurrection he will be the first one to rise from the dead.

The above distinctions are special to him.

From Sūrah  al-An'ām 6: 163

Although it is a divine name, the Qur'ān mentions it as the Prophet Muḥammad's name as well.

75

THE LAST ONE

THAT the Prophet Muḥammad (peace be upon him) is the last Messenger of Allah is common knowledge. He happens to be the leader of the last community of believers.

His being the Final Prophet is a great distinction. For his teachings are valid for all time and place. Being the followers and bearers of his message, it is our bounden duty to profess and practise faith as he taught it and as best we can.

From Daylāmi  Al-Firdaws bi Ma'thūr al-Khiṭāb

Although it is a divine name, the Qur'ān mentions it as the Prophet Muḥammad's name as well.

76

الظَّاهِرُ

THE EVIDENT ONE

ALLAH promised the Prophet Muḥammad (peace be upon him) in the Qur'ān that He will make Islam prevail over all other religions (al-Ṣaff 61: 9, al-Tawbah 9: 33 and al-Fatḥ 48: 28). His promise came true and the Prophet's name and mission spread far and wide on an unprecedented scale in a short time.

We should thank and glorify Allah for having granted such eminence to the Prophet (peace be upon him). Also, we should strive in upholding and reinforcing the glory of Islam which, in turn, will keep aloft the Prophet's mission.

From Sūrah al-Ṣaff 61: 9

Although it is a divine name, the Qur'ān mentions it as the Prophet Muḥammad's name as well.

77

HE WHO POSSESSED UNSEEN KNOWLEDGE

As the Messenger of Allah, the Prophet Muḥammad (peace be upon him) was imparted by Allah some special knowledge, especially of the unseen. During his night journey ascension (*miʿrāj*), referred to in Sūrah al-Isrā' 17: 1, he witnessed some of the signs of Allah.

His Ḥadīth corpus testifies to some special knowledge granted to him by Allah.

From Qāḍī ʿAyāḍ Kitāb al-Shifā'

78

رَحْمَةُ لِلعَالَمِينَ

MERCY TO THE WORLDS

From Sūrah al-Anbiyā' 21: 107

THE Qur'ān proclaims that Allah sent down the Prophet Muḥammad (peace be upon him) as mercy to all people of the worlds (al-Anbiyā' 21: 107). His kindness and mercy even towards his enemies, who were after his blood, bears out the truth of the above Qur'ānic assertion. Throughout his life he did not hit anyone, what to say of killing. It is on record that when the Makkan unbelievers' persecution turned almost intolerable, someone suggested to the Prophet (peace be upon him) that he may curse them. To this he replied that his advent constituted mercy for the worlds. It did not, therefore, befit him to curse even die-hard unbelievers.

His mercy was reflected at its sharpest in his improving the plight of women, widows, orphans and the poor. His overflowing love for children also stemmed from his mercy.

This role model should set us on the path of love and kindness for our fellow human beings.

79

HE WHO ALLOWED THINGS

From Sūrah  al-Aʿrāf 7: 157

GUIDED by divine revelation, the Prophet Muḥammad (peace be upon him) declared things lawful. So doing, he acted on the Qur'ānic verse (al-Aʿrāf 7: 157) which authorized him to brand things as lawful or unlawful. The laws enacted by him, in line with the Qur'ān, went a long way in providing relief to people who had been oppressed by restrictions imposed by clergy.

The Prophet (peace be upon him) enjoyed the prerogative of pronouncing things as lawful or otherwise. It is yet another proof of his exalted status in the Islamic scheme of things and in Allah's reckoning.

80

HE WHO FORBADE THINGS

On Allah's authority the Prophet Muḥammad (peace be upon him) forbade unlawful things. According to the Qur'ān, Allah had granted the following mandate to him: "*He enjoins upon them what is good and forbids them what is evil. He makes clean things lawful to them and prohibits all unlawful things and removes from them their burdens and shackles which were upon them.*" (al-Aʿrāf 7: 157)

Going by the above, it is clear that only the Prophet (peace be upon him) enjoyed the authority to declare something unlawful. No one else is authorized to do so. Islam has no room for clergy. Nowadays, the *ʿUlamā'* and jurists may arrive at consensus, in the light of the rulings by the Qur'ān and Sunnah, for declaring something unlawful in today's context.

However, it was the Prophet's special privilege conferred upon him by Allah.

From Sūrah al-Aʿrāf 7: 157

81

HE WHO GAVE COMMANDS

As the Messenger of Allah and as the head of the Muslim state and community, the Prophet Muḥammad (peace be upon him) issued commands which were readily followed. To be more precise, as the Qur'ān states: "*He commands them (mankind) what is good and forbids them what is evil.*" (al-Aʿrāf 7: 157)

In Islam, obedience to him stands for obedience to Allah. His sayings and practices, known as Ḥadīth and Sunnah respectively, are therefore a primary source of Islam. On behalf of Allah, he enacted Islamic laws which have been in force since his era to this day.

From Sūrah al-Aʿrāf 7: 157

HE WHO FORBADE THINGS

The Qur'ān assigns the following main functions to the Prophet (peace be upon him): of inviting people to Islam, of giving good news to those who embrace truth and of warning those who reject truth. We are further directed: "*Refrain from whatever he forbids you.*" (al-Ḥashr 59: 7) He forbade, on Allah's directive, all which is unlawful, obscene and unwholesome. It was part of his Prophetic assignment to prohibit all corrupting things and to remove the shackles which oppressed humanity.

As Muslims it is our bounden duty to shun all that the Prophet (peace be upon him) forbade. In this lies our eternal success.

From Sunan al-Ḥashr 59: 7

83

الشَّكُورُ

HE WHO THANKED ALLAH

From Sūrah al-Zumar 39: 66

ALLAH'S directive for all of us is: "*Serve Allah alone and be among those who thank Him.*" (al-Zumar 39: 66) It was the Prophet Muḥammad (peace be upon him) who excelled over everyone in thanking Allah profusely and fervently. ʿĀ'ishah, the Prophet's wife, informs that he used to stand in prayers for most of the night. Once she asked him as to why he prayed to Allah so profusely, while Allah had promised to overlook his lapses and to admit him to His mercy. To this he replied: "Should I not be a thankful servant of Him?" (Al-Bukhārī, *Kitāb al-Tahajjud*: 1,078).

The high standard set by the Prophet (peace be upon him) for thanking and glorifying Allah should be emulated by us. In this lies our success and happiness in both the worlds.

Although it is a divine name, the Qur'ān mentions it as the Prophet Muḥammad's name as well.

THE CLOSE ONE

THE Qur'ān states that the Prophet Muḥammad (peace be upon him) was very close to his Companions. (al-Aḥzāb 33: 6) His elevation as the Final Messenger of Allah, his receiving the invaluable eternal book of guidance, the Qur'ān, and his night journey (*mi'rāj*) are some pointers to his proximity with Allah.

More remarkably, he fulfilled perfectly what was expected of him as being close to fellow Muslims and to Allah.

We can learn much from the Prophet's blessed life how to strike a perfect balance between our obligations to Allah and to human beings.

From Sūrah al-Aḥzāb 33: 6

HE WHO TURNED TO ALLAH

From Sūrah Saba' 34: 9

TRUE faith prompts man to turn in repentance to his Lord. The Prophet Muḥammad (peace be upon him) exemplified this trait at its best. He spent hours at night, entreating to Allah, seeking His forgiveness and rewards not only for himself and his family, but also for the whole community and mankind. At times, his wife 'Ā'ishah marvelled at his long hours of devotion, especially in the early morning, as a result of which his feet were swollen.

As Allah loves His servants' repentance, we should turn to Him, imploring for His forgiveness and rewards.

HE WHO WAS FULL OF VIRTUES

BEING the intensive form of *barr* (the virtuous), it is used of the Prophet Muḥammad (peace be upon him). Rather, he is rightly hailed as *Imām al-Bārrīn* (Leader of the virtuous). Thc significance of the appellation *al-Barr* comes out from this Ḥadīth in which the Prophet (peace be upon him) is found saying:

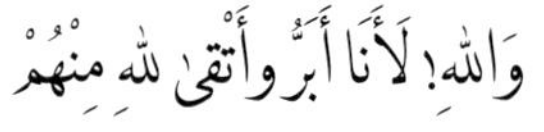
وَاللهِ! لَأَنَا أَبَرُّ وأَتْقَى للهِ مِنْهُمْ

(البخاري، كتاب الشركة)

By Allah! I am the most virtuous and the most God-fearing one.

(Al-Bukhārī, *Kitāb al-Shirkah*: 2,371)

From Sūrah al-Qalam 68: 4

87

THE PREACHER

From Sūrah al-Mā'idah 5: 97

The Qur'ān entrusted the Prophet Muḥammad (peace be upon him) with the mission of delivering the Divine message. Rather, it states: "*The Messenger has no other responsibility but to convey clearly (Allah's commands).*" (al-Nūr 24: 57)

It is common knowledge that he acquitted himself well of this job. Not only was Islam firmly established in his lifetime in vast areas of the world, it soon spread far and wide, thanks to his effective preaching. Furthermore, he put in place an elaborate mechanism for preaching Islam in all time to come.

The Prophet's strategy of preaching and his commitment to this cause are worth emulating. We should dedicate ourselves to his noble mission of preaching Islam.

88

ṬĀ SĪN

ṬĀ SĪN is an abbreviated letter which prefaces Sūrah al-Naml. While it is hard to establish the precise meaning of this and other Qur'ānic abbreviated letters, some scholars such as Zurqānī, Nasafī, Ṣāliḥī and Sakhāwī are of the view that *Ṭā Sīn* is one of the names of the Prophet Muḥammad (peace be upon him).

From Sūrah al-Naml 27: 1

89

حمٓ

HĀ MĪM

QUR'ĀNIC Sūrahs 40–46 open with the abbreviated letters: *Ḥā Mīm*. The exact meaning of these abbreviated letters which appear at the beginning of certain Qur'ānic Sūrahs is not known to us. Some scholars take these to be the names of Allah while others designate these to be the names of the Prophet Muḥammad (peace be upon him) or of the Qur'ān.

According to Māwardī, Sakhāwī, Shīrāzī and Ismāʿīl Ḥaqqī, *Ḥā Mīm* signifies the Prophet's name, alluding to some special favours bestowed by Allah on him.

90

الحَسِيبُ

HE WHO SUFFICED

PROPHET Muḥammad (peace be upon him) sufficed well for all the needs of the Muslim community, as is recorded in this Hadith:

He sufficed for his community: (Al-Suyūṭī, *Al-Riyāḍ al-Anīqah:* 143). Combined in his illustrious personality were the facets of a great statesman, spiritual master, military strategist and social reformer. He influenced all aspects of community life. In view of his sterling qualities everyone turned to him for help and advice. In the Next Life too, he will rescue the Muslim community by Allah's permission to him for intercession.

THE CLOSER ONE

From Sūrah al-Aḥzāb 33: 6

ACCORDING to the Qur'ān, the Prophet (peace be upon him) is closer to believers than their own selves. The same truth is reiterated in this Ḥadīth:

مَا مِنْ مُؤْمِنٍ اِلاَّ وَأَنَا أَوْلَىٰ النَّاسَ بِهِ فِي الدُّنْيَا وَالآخِرَة

(البخاري ، كتاب تفسير القرآن)

In both this world and the Next I am closer to believers than their own selves

(Al-Bukhārī, *Kitāb Tafsīr al-Qur'ān:* 4,503)

We should fulfil the obligations arising out of this close relationship. Our obedience to the Prophet (peace be upon him) should demonstrate our attachment to him.

92

THE MOST GENEROUS AMONG PEOPLE

IBN ʿAbbās, an eminent Companion, relates that: "The Prophet (peace be upon him) was the most generous among people in doing good" (Al-Bukhārī, *Kitāb Bad' al-Waḥy*: 1,902).

In all acts of devotional worship, charity and virtues, the Prophet (peace be upon him) excelled over everyone. He never turned away any needy person. Nor did he refuse to cooperate in something good and noble.

Going by his example, we should be kind and generous to everyone.

93

أَفْضَلُ الأَنْبِيَاءِ

THE DIVINELY FAVOURED PROPHET

From Sūrah  al-Nisā' 4: 113

THE Qur'ān announces that Allah's grace unto the Prophet Muḥammad (peace be upon him) is immense. (al-Nisā' 4: 113) The above point is elucidated in the Ḥadīth report in which the Prophet (peace be upon him) spells out his six distinctions which make him stand out above other Prophet's: (i) He was granted pithy words; (ii) his awe overwhelmed people; (iii) spoils of war were made lawful for him; (iv) the entire planet earth was declared clean for prayers for him and believers; (v) he was sent as mercy unto the humanity; (vi) he is the seal of Prophets.

In view of his excellence we should be all the more obedient to his teachings.

THE HONOURED ONE

IN view of his accomplishments the Prophet Muḥammad (peace be upon him), no doubt, happens to be the most honoured person in history of all time. Allah conferred upon him many honours and he has always been held in great esteem by Muslims over the centuries.

His distinctions are many and varied. More importantly, he is without a match in several respects. For example, as illustrated by the American author, Michael Hart in his book, *The* 100, the Prophet Muḥammad (peace be upon him) holds the unique distinction of being the most influential person in history.

From Sūrah al-Ḥāqqah 69: 40

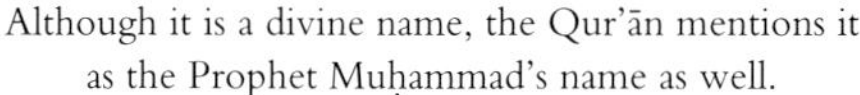
Although it is a divine name, the Qur'ān mentions it as the Prophet Muḥammad's name as well.

95

إِمَامُ الأَنْبِيَاءِ

LEADER OF THE PROPHETS

From Ibn Taimiyyah Majmū' al-Fatāwā: 1/2,431

PROPHET Muḥammad (peace be upon him) will enjoy an exalted status in the grand assembly on the Day of Judgement. He informs: "Without any pride let me tell you that on the Day of Judgement I will be the leader of the Prophets, their spokesperson and intercessor".

We should take pride in being members of the community of such a distinguished Prophet. However, its binds us at the same time to the task of propagating his mission as best as we can.

96

البَرُّ

THE RIGHTEOUS ONE

In recognition of the Prophet Muḥammad's exceptional goodness the Qur'ān cites his life and conduct as the perfect example to be followed by all down the ages, rather until the end of time: "*Surely there is a good example for you in the Messenger of Allah for all those who look forward to Allah and the Last Day and remember Allah much.*" (al-Aḥzāb 33: 21) Not only ordinary believers, even those who are devout are asked by the Qur'ān to emulate the Prophet's example. This points to his exceptionally high and noteworthy standard of piety.

May Allah guide us to this model.

From Sūrah  al-Aḥzāb 33: 21

Although it is a divine name, the Qur'ān mentions it as the Prophet Muḥammad's name as well.

97

THE PIOUS ONE

From al-Dārimī Sunan: 92

The Prophet's piety is exemplary. Both in acts of devotional worship and his fair dealings with fellow human beings, he set a new record of piety. Works on his life document several inspiring examples of his piety. The Qur'ān records that while hiding in a cave, on his emigration from Makkah to Madinah, as his Makkan enemies had reached almost the mouth of the cave, he did not lose his poise and comforted his Companion, Abū Bakr, telling him that they had Allah's protection.

Another outstanding proof of his piety is his frugal lifestyle, notwithstanding the vast riches which had been at his disposal, especially in the last phase of his Prophetic career.

98

THE DEFENDER

The Prophet (peace be upon him) stands out as the defender of faith in the true sense of the word. First he protected the Islamic faith, which was in its infancy, from the unbelievers' onslaught. Their concerted opposition, persecution and even well-equipped attacks and invasions did not and could not uproot the fledgling faith. Moreover, he saw to it that the true faith was not diluted or corrupted in the least. He trained his Companions so well that they carried out his message zealously, which established Islam once and for all in major parts of the world.

From al-Bukhārī Kitāb al-Buyūʿ: 2,125

99

THE WISE ONE

The Qur'ān states that Allah granted wisdom to the Prophet Muḥammad (peace be upon him) and that he instructed believers in the same (al-Isrā' 17: 39 and al-Jumu'ah 62: 2). His wisdom is reflected also in his pithy sayings which constitute the Ḥadīth corpus. His decisions as the leader of the Muslim community both in war and peace, his statesmanship as the head of the Islamic state in Madinah and his advice and counselling to his community members demonstrate his sagacity.

We should draw upon this treasure documented in the Sīrah and Ḥadīth for our better prospects in both the worlds.

From Sūrah al-Isrā' 17: 39

Although it is a divine name, the Qur'ān mentions it as the Prophet Muḥammad's name as well.

INDEX

Excellent Names and Attributes of the Prophet Muḥammad (peace be upon him)

21	Al-Rasūl	الرَّسُولُ
22	Al-Nabī	النَّبِيُّ
23	Ṭā Hā	طَٰهَ
24	Yā Sīn	يَٰسِ
25	Al-Muzzammil	المُزَّمِّلُ
26	Al-Muddaththir	المُدَّثِّرُ
27	Al-Shafī‘	الشَّفِيعُ
28	Al-Khalīl	الخَلِيلُ
29	Kalīm Allāh	كَلِيمُ اللهِ
30	Ḥabīb Allāh	حَبِيبُ اللهِ
31	Al-Muṣṭafā	المُصْطَفَىٰ
32	Al-Murtaḍā	المُرْتَضَىٰ
33	Al-Mujtabā	المُجْتَبَىٰ
34	Al-Nāṣir	النَّاصِرُ
35	Al-Manṣūr	المَنْصُورُ
36	Al-Qā’im	القَائِمُ
37	Al-Ḥāfiẓ	الحَافِظُ
38	Al-Shahīd	الشَّهِيدُ
39	Al-‘Ādil	العَادِلُ
40	Al-Ḥākim	الحَاكِمُ
41	Al-Nūr	النُّورُ
42	Al-Ḥujjah	الحُجَّةُ

43	Al-Burhān	البُرْهَانُ
44	Abū Al-Mu'minīn	أَبُو الـمُؤْمِنِـينَ
45	Al-Matīn	الـمَتِينُ
46	Al-Mudhakkir	الـمُذَكِّرُ
47	Al-Wāʿiẓ	الوَاعِظُ
48	Al-Amīn	الأَمِينُ
49	Al-Ṣādiq	الصَّادِقُ
50	Al-Muṣaddiq	الـمُصَدِّقُ
51	Al-Nāṭiq bi'l-Ḥaqq	النَّاطِقُ بِالـحَق
52	Al-Ṣāḥib	الصَّاحِبُ
53	Al-Qurashī	القُرَشِيُّ
54	Al-Ummī	الأُمِّيُّ
55	Al-ʿAzīz	العَزِيزُ
56	Al-Ra'ūf	الرَّؤُوفُ
57	Al-Raḥīm	الرَّحِيمُ
58	Al-Yatīm	اليَتِيمُ
59	Al-Ghanī	الغَنِـيُّ
60	Al-Jawād	الـجَوَادُ
61	Al-Fattāḥ	الفَتَّاحُ
62	Al-Mā'mūn	الـمَأمُونُ
63	Al-Ṭayyib	الطَّيِّبُ
64	Al-Ṭāhir	الطَّاهِرُ

الـمُطَهِّرُ	Al-Muṭahhir	65
خَطِيبُ الأَنْبِيَاءِ	Khaṭīb Al-Anbiyā’	66
الفَصِيحُ	Al-Faṣīḥ	67
السَّيِّدُ	Al-Sayyid	68
الـمُنَقِّي	Al-Munaqqī	69
إِمَامُ الـمُتَّقِينَ	Imām Al-Mutaqqīn	70
الشَّافِي	Al-Shāfī	71
الـمُتَوَسِّطُ	Al-Mutawasiṭ	72
السَّابِقُ	Al-Sābiq	73
الـمُقْتَصِدُ	Al-Muqtaṣid	74
الـمَهْدِيُّ	Al-Mahdī	75
الـحَقُّ	Al-Ḥaqq	76
الـمُبِينُ	Al-Mubīn	77
الأَوَّلُ	Al-Awwal	78
الآخِرُ	Al-Ākhir	79
الظَّاهِرُ	Al-Ẓāhir	80
البَاطِنُ	Al-Bāṭin	81
رَحْـمَةٌ لِلعَالَـمِينَ	Raḥmatul lil-ʿĀlamīn	82
الـمُحَلِّلُ	Al-Muḥallil	84
الـمُحَرِّمُ	Al-Muḥarrim	85
الآمِرُ	Al-Āmir	86
النَّاهِي	Al-Nāhī	87

NOTES

NOTES

NOTES